D1410625

MEAT from Ranch to Table

MEAT from

Ranch to Table

Written and Illustrated by
WALTER BUEHR

WILLIAM MORROW AND COMPANY

New York   1956

To
Nina and Laurie

CONTENTS

Page

Who Eats Meat? 11

Meat in Early Europe 24

Meat in Early America 33

Meat on the Move 38

The Meat Industry Today 63

    1. Cattle 65

    2. Sheep 76

    3. Hogs 80

Inside the Slaughterhouse 86

MEAT from Ranch to Table

Who Eats Meat?

As evening approaches and tantalizing odors begin to drift through the house from the kitchen, that old familiar cry of anticipation arises: "What's for dinner?" Nine times out of ten, what the questioner really wants to know is: "What kind of *meat* are we having for dinner?"

Almost everybody who picks up a menu at a restaurant decides first on his meat course, before even thinking of soup, vegetables, or dessert. Restaurants are often named for their special meat cuts; such places as Ye Olde Choppe House or Paddy's Steak House are familiar sights in any city, but whoever heard of Ye Cauliflower Inne or Mamie's Spinach House? There's no denying it—meat is king at the table.

In ancient times people depended on meat even more than they do now, so in those days they were willing to bite into almost anything that didn't bite back. They were brave souls; besides the meats we use, they cooked dogs, cats, goats, oxen, swans, peacocks, porpoises, seals, camels, and horses, and ate them, too. In some places they still do.

The word *meat* can be applied to all animal food, including fish and fowl, but usually when we talk about meat today we mean the kind that comes from three domestic animals. Most important of these, from the point of view of world-wide consumption, are hogs. From them we get pork chops, roasts, sausages, ham, and bacon. Cattle (cows, bulls, and steers) come next. From calves we get veal and from grown cattle beef, which we eat as steaks, roasts, hamburger, stews, and sausages—though sausage meat is more often made from pork or a mixture of beef and pork. Last on the list are sheep. Mutton, the meat of grown sheep, is well liked in England and Australia, but Americans prefer the meat of lambs, in the form of lamb stew, leg of lamb, and lamb chops.

Although we Americans all like pork, beef, and lamb, our tastes differ somewhat. People in the East like beef best, while pork is the favorite in the South. More lamb is eaten in the cities along the east and west coasts than inland, and only in the largest cities is there much call for veal.

Our appetites change with the seasons; we usually eat more meat in cool weather than in hot. What our grandfathers ate also has a lot to do with what we like. In Italian neighborhoods butchers have to carry highly spiced sausages like pepperoni, while German or Dutch sections demand *Bratwurst,* for instance.

Some areas like lean pork sausages; others, such as New England, want more fat in them.

The Southwest likes its meat hot with spices, but in the North the flavoring has to be mild. Even holiday tastes vary. While the rest of the country feasts on roast turkey or goose at Christmas, the Spanish-speaking sections of the big Eastern cities would consider their holiday a failure if it lacked a baked suckling pig with crisp, crackling skin.

We Americans eat a lot of meat every year. In 1954 our average was about 155 pounds per person: 79 pounds of beef, 10 pounds of veal, 4½ pounds of lamb and mutton, and 62 pounds of

pork. In only three other countries are the plates piled higher with meat than in ours. Australians eat 205 pounds of meat per person every year, Argentinians 300 pounds, and New Zealanders a whopping 321 pounds. In those countries, however, meat raising is the main industry, and so meat is cheap and plentiful.

Most of us have never given a thought to the long-range planning, the knowledge, care, and skill, and the enormous amount of land, labor, equipment, and money it takes to produce the meat for our dinner tables, and what a risky business it is.

Raising meat animals, fattening them for the market, slaughtering, and cutting up the meat and shipping it to the butcher shops form a continuous process. Ranchers and hog raisers cannot increase or cut down their production as an automobile manufacturer can. Calves and lambs and pigs keep being born each year regardless of market prices, and they have to be fed every day. The man who raises them must sell his stock when they are ready or risk losing money on them because of the cost of extra feed and labor.

Meat packers who buy the animals from the stock raisers have to be shrewd businessmen; they must guess, and guess right most of the time, how much meat each part of the country will buy. Once it is shipped, meat must be sold quickly, because more and more of it keeps coming along the endless chain of supply. Besides, some kinds of meat will spoil after a few days even when kept chilled.

Meat prices rise and fall, not because they are controlled by some central power, but for many other reasons. If there is a long spell without rain on the cattle range, the grass dries up, the animals grow thin, many of them die, and fewer young are born. This, strangely enough, can make prices either rise or fall. If enough cattlemen have to sell their cattle to avoid seeing them starve to death, so many animals may arrive at the stockyards at the same time that they flood the market. Then competition among the sellers is so brisk that prices are forced down. If, on the other hand, conditions are so bad that only a few herds are fit to ship to the stockyards, buyers must compete to get enough animals to keep the packing houses going, and therefore prices go up.

Good pasture and a large corn crop may bring heavy shipments of steers to market and depress prices. Uneven supply throughout the year also causes price changes. Most range animals are born in the spring of the year. Nature planned it that way so that the young do not have to face winter storms on the open range until they are at least six months old. Then, too, in the spring there is plenty of tender young grass for the mothers, which means plenty of milk for the babies.

Because young meat animals are usually born at about the same time, they also mature at the same time. This creates peaks and valleys in the "meat-supply calendar." Most calves and lambs arrive in the market in September and October,

most pigs in the late fall and early winter, and most beef cattle from September to December. At these peak times meat is naturally cheaper than at the low point for deliveries.

We are a large nation—over 160 million of us—and we eat lots of meat. To supply our meat and dairy needs there is one cow for every two people, and half of the cattle are beef animals. There are two fifths as many hogs and two fifths as many sheep as there are people, but most sheep are kept for their wool rather than for food.

Five of the six million farms and ranches in the United States raise some cattle. Four million farms raise hogs, and six hundred thousand farms grow sheep. Each year over a hundred million cattle, hogs, and sheep—about twenty-four billion pounds of meat—are shipped to the packing houses to be turned into steaks, chops, roasts, and sausages.

Look at the map of the United States. The Mississippi River divides it into two parts.

THE WES

GRAZING LAND

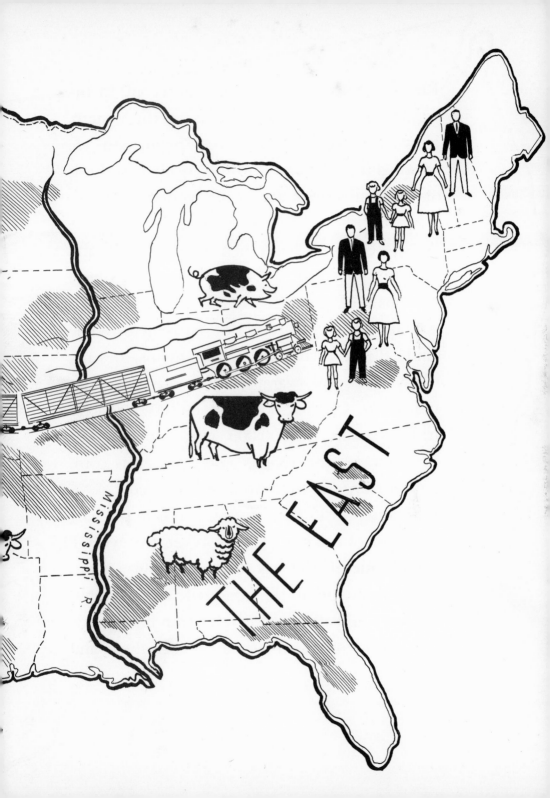

THE EAST

Mississippi R.

Roughly two thirds of the country are in the western part and one third is in the eastern. However, two thirds of our population are crowded into the eastern third, while two thirds of all our livestock are in the western part.

Most of the animals are born and raised in the West, because it has much more grazing land and a cow or sheep needs a lot of pasture. A little over half of the area of our country—1,061, 000,000 acres—is useful for farming of some kind; the rest consists of mountains, deserts, lakes, rivers, and swamps, or is covered by cities and towns. Of the good land, 600,000,000 acres are in pasture, 85,000,000 acres grow hay or other forage, and 135,000,000 acres grow corn, oats, barley, and soybeans used for feed.

Because most of our population is in the East and most of the stock in the West, the average hog or side of beef has to travel about a thousand miles to get to the housewife's kitchen. No rancher could afford to drive or ship his animals a thousand miles and then butcher them and

peddle the meat to his customers. Somebody with skill, equipment, and capital has to
buy the stock from the meat raiser, butcher the
meat, and distribute it to all the cities and towns
full of meat-hungry people. This somebody is the
meat packer, and he does the job with such good
planning and so little waste that butcher shops
from Maine to Florida and from New York to
San Francisco always have plenty of good, tender meats at prices their customers can afford.

Meat in Early Europe

We learn from ancient evidence that meat played an important part in the food supplies of our forefathers. Figures painted and engraved on the walls of caves show that prehistoric man hunted, for their flesh, such animals as bison, lions, and wild pigs.

The Phoenicians did not eat beef or pork, but they enjoyed a nice broiled dog. The Israelites and Egyptians were meat eaters, but their priests forbade pork, probably because they had learned how quickly pork spoiled in their hot climate. The Romans, however, liked pork (they knew as many as fifty pork dishes), but they were not allowed to eat goat's meat, which was considered unclean. Before Rome was conquered by the barbarians, its government had established many sanitary slaughterhouses and butcher stalls. Even as far back as the time of Homer, the Greeks salted meat and made sausages.

In the fourteenth and fifteenth centuries the people of Europe were eating meat, game, fowl, and fish in many strange forms, and these foods formed almost the entire menu. What few vegetables they knew were used mostly to garnish and flavor the meat dishes.

Medieval butchers almost always slaughtered in the autumn, because when the grass died there was little fodder to keep animals alive through the winter. Usually only enough beasts for breeding were saved. This meant that in the fall there was a great deal of fresh meat available which nobody knew how to keep from spoiling except by salting it or pickling it in brine. For a few days everybody ate as much fresh meat as he could hold and then had to be satisfied with salt meat until the next autumn.

Fresh meat began to taste unpleasant in a very short time, so medieval cooks flavored their dishes with aromatic herbs and spices to disguise the taste. When they weren't serving enormous roasts, they often combined as many different kinds of food in one dish as they could think of, chopping and grinding them and then turning the whole mixture into a mushy paste with a mortar and pestle. The main course for Sunday dinner at a baron's castle might contain pork, beef, goose, and fish, all chopped up together and mashed. Into this paste would go egg whites, sliced pears and oranges, grapes, almonds, and acorns, also mashed fine. Any cook considered himself disgraced if the diners could tell what was in a dish, so into the mortar went liberal dashes of wine and cider and a sprinkling of

spices, such as cinnamon, cloves, mace, saffron, and ginger. The whole mixture was then boiled for several hours and finally served triumphantly to the unfortunate victims at the table.

For really important banquets the cooks, of course, took extra pains. The medieval cook seemed more interested in how a dish looked than how it tasted. A whole roast pig, with an apple in its mouth, raisins for eyes, and a wreath of holly leaves, fruits, and berries around its neck was a usual holiday treat, but those fifteenth-century cooks also went in for much fancier fare. After a peacock had been carefully skinned, stuffed, and roasted, the skin, with all the feathers, was replaced. The peacock's long tail was gracefully rearranged, and a brandy-soaked feather was put into its bill and set alight. The chief cook himself then carried in the tray holding this work of art.

One cook, in charge of a great banquet for royalty, determined to outdo all the splendors of the past. Into a cleaned peacock he stuffed a cleaned

and boned goose; into the goose he put a boned fat hen, and into the hen a partridge. He fitted a boned quail into the partridge and a lark inside the quail. The heavily stuffed peacock was then roasted and dressed in its own skin once more. The proud cook presented his masterpiece to the diners and, before the royal guest's startled eyes, carved slices consisting of the meat of six kinds of birds.

Late in the fifteenth century it became more usual to serve baked and boiled meats without mashing them up. This was just about the time when the fork came into use; previously only knives and spoons were known. Without a fork, a diner could not hold his meat on the plate to cut it, so any roast meat had to be cut by the carver into slices small enough to be handled with the fingers. By 1587 it became the fashion to serve a great platter of many different kinds of meat. Such a platter was called a "met."

There are many stories of King Henry VIII of England and his love of good food. One day at a banquet, the cook placed before him a juicy loin of beef, done to a turn and with just the right amount of fat. As the delicious fragrance reached the King's nostrils he rose, drew his sword, and laid it across the meat, saying, "I dub thee Sir

Loin," as if he were creating a knight. Today we still call this cut of beef a sirloin.

Many of the spices that medieval cooks felt they must have to garnish their dishes and also to disguise the flavor of slightly spoiled meat came from India and the Far East. Spices were rare and costly, because they had to travel so far, by caravan and ship, and because many cargoes were lost to bandits and pirates. One of the main reasons fifteenth-century adventurers and explorers set out on their voyages was to find a new and shorter sea route to India and so make their fortunes by bringing back shiploads of these much-wanted spices. In a roundabout way, we can give meat some of the credit for the discovery of America!

Meat in Early America

The Spaniards, who were among the earliest explorers in America, introduced domestic meat animals in this continent. These explorers always tried to colonize and civilize the new lands, so that the territory they annexed should remain Spanish. A Spanish expedition included not only soldiers in steel helmets and breastplates, but also priests, farmers, and herdsmen. Besides the horses of the cavalry, there would be small herds of Andalusian cattle, swine, and sheep, as well as chickens and ducks. On his second trip to the

West Indies in 1493, Columbus brought over domestic animals with him, but he never reached the mainland. The American savages had to wait nearly fifty years longer to see their first horse, cow, pig, or sheep.

The Indians had always lived mostly on wild game trapped or shot with arrows. When a hunter killed a bison or a deer, the whole tribe gorged on the fresh meat; what was left over they either jerked (cut in strips and hung on poles in the sun to dry) or smoked over a low fire, to keep it from spoiling. The Indians never thought of taming and penning up any of the native animals to be killed and eaten later.

The Spaniards already had settlements in the West Indies and Mexico when Hernando de Soto's fleet of nine small ships, loaded with six hundred armor-clad cavalry and foot soldiers landed in Tampa Bay, Florida, in 1539, to conquer and colonize North America. Part of their cargo was a squealing, grunting herd of thirteen hogs, the forebears of our Southern razorback hogs. They were the first domestic animals to set foot on American soil.

De Soto and his band made an amazing march up from Florida and through what are now Georgia and the Carolinas and Tennessee and west to the Mississippi River, struggling through swamps and almost impassable wildernesses, over mountains and across deep rivers.

Sometimes the Indians were friendly and fed them, but often the Spaniards had to fight them, on empty bellies. When things got desperate and no other food was in sight, De Soto ordered some of the pigs slaughtered, but each of his men got only a half pound a day. Although by this time the pig herd had increased enormously, De Soto wanted to save both the old swine and the young piglets to help start the colony he expected to found.

During a fierce battle with the Indians in the winter of 1540-41, the Spaniards set fire to the Indian village of straw huts, but lost most of their own supplies and equipment in the flames. Of the many descendants of the original thirteen swine brought ashore at Tampa Bay, only a hundred escaped the fire.

After a year spent wandering in the wilderness west of the Mississippi, the Spaniards returned to the river, where De Soto died. After great hardships the expedition made its way along the Texas coast to the Spanish colonies in Mexico. All along their line of march occasional pigs strayed from the herd, and their offspring brought the first juicy hams and pork chops to America.

Later, another expedition, commanded by Hernando Cortes, landed on a beach near the present city of Vera Cruz, Mexico, with a detachment of soldiers, sixteen horses, and seven small black, long-horned Andalusian cattle, including a bull. This expedition wandered up the coast and into what is now Texas, where they settled down and began raising the first beef cattle in North America—the forerunners of the famous Texas longhorns.

Other meat animals imported during the early days came ashore from the harbors of the Atlantic coast. Newfoundland and Nova Scotia traded for hogs with Portuguese traders as early as 1553, while the Jamestown colony in Virginia received cattle from England in May, 1611.

The Plymouth Rock Pilgrims brought no domestic animals at all; they were mostly city folk who knew so little about raising their own food, either animal or vegetable, that they would have starved during the first hard years without the help of friendly Indians. Finally, after three years, it occurred to somebody in the colony to bring in some cattle, and in 1624 the ship *Charity* landed three Devonshire cows and a bull. The Dutchmen who settled New Amsterdam (New York) were more practical; they brought with them 103 black-and-white Dutch cattle.

Meat on the Move

The New England cattle industry began to grow rapidly after the middle of the seventeenth century. Because there was no way of shipping butchered meat or storing it under refrigeration, cattle from Vermont and New Hampshire were driven to Boston and other towns for slaughter. The first cattle drive on the Old Bay Path between Springfield and Boston occurred in 1665. It was conducted by John Pynchon, son of William Pynchon, the first commercial meat raiser in the colonies.

From the farms where they were raised, the animals were driven to the cities along the public roads. Horsemen or coaches often had to pull up in the ditch when they saw a cloud of choking dust approaching. When this drew nearer it might reveal a herd of bellowing cattle, tossing their horns in panic as the mounted herdsmen cracked their long whips and their dogs barked excitedly. Or it might turn out to be a herd of hogs, grunting balefully as the herd boys poked

them with long sticks and the dogs snapped at their hams, or a peaceful flock of sheep stupidly following their belled leader (called the Judas goat), which was leading them to their death. Even flocks of geese were often driven along the turnpike during those slow-paced days before the automobile.

Once in town, the animals were penned up and quickly butchered, while the town crier went about the streets with clanging bell, crying, "Fresh meat now at the butcher's! Get your fresh meat!" Townspeople came from every direction to get their fresh-killed roasts or chops and hurry home to cook them before they spoiled. It was feast or famine in those early days—either more fresh meat than a body could eat, or none at all until the next herd was driven into town.

On the farms it was the same story. The farmers did their own butchering, saving and curing the hides to make shoes and harness, trying out the lard from the animals' fat, and salting and pickling pork and beef. But they, too, could only

expect to have fresh meat for a couple of days after a butchering.

As the cities grew and settlers moved farther and farther west, distances grew too great for the herds to be driven along the dusty or muddy roads to the towns where the meat was to be eaten. Local farmers or butchers began setting up small slaughterhouses where they could cut up and salt the meat from the herds of neighboring farms and ship the barrels of salt pork and beef to the cities. Some, taking a lesson from the Indians, dried or smoked their meat and learned to improve the flavor by adding spices and herbs. Others made casings out of the intestines of the beasts and filled them with ground-up meat, corn meal, and spices, and then cooked or smoked them and so had sausages to sell. These early packing houses flourished for two reasons. The neighboring farmers who supplied the animals had to drive them only a short distance. And the packers could ship their kegs of salt meat long distances by wagon or boat much more easily than live animals could be transported.

At last the railroads began spreading slowly across the nation. By the 1870's, farmers were able to ship their stock by rail to the packer from points much farther away than those from which they could drive them on the hoof. The steel rails soon reached beyond the settled Middle West, crossed the Mississippi, and began to tap the vast, empty western prairies.

Though hogs cannot digest grass and must therefore be raised on farms where corn is grown for their feed, cattle and sheep can live on the wild grasses of the open range. Each animal needs a good many acres of pasturage (depending on the abundance of grass), and so a large herd has to have a great deal of range. This is why the western prairies are such a fine place to raise great numbers of cattle and sheep inexpensively.

Only the lack of transportation had held back the development of meat raising in the West. The coming of the railroads changed all that. When the stock trains began running from Abilene and Dodge City, Kansas, the ranchers at last had a way of getting their meat to the consumer. So, in the early 1870's, the great days of western ranching began, with all the excitement of roundups, branding, and great trail herds. These were the days glorified by the movie western.

The early ranchers did not need to own land. There were thousands of square miles of government land which they could use free or for a small fee. All they needed was a small home ranch as headquarters, a herd of cattle, a few cowboys, and a string of saddle horses. Their cattle were distributed over areas where they could find good grass and water, and left to take care of themselves as long as there was feed. Sometimes they had to be moved to better pasturage, and in

winter the herds were usually quartered in some sheltered valley. If the snow got so deep that the cattle could not paw down to the grass, the rancher had to spread hay around to keep them alive until spring.

Because there were no fences on the range, the cattle roamed at will and so, of course, the herds

were all mixed together. Without some way of marking them, nobody could have told which cows were his, so every calf was branded with a distinctive and permanent mark, which was burned into the hide over one hip.

Branding was one of the main reasons for the roundups, which were usually held in both spring and fall. At roundup time every ranch for many miles around sent out a team of its riders under a foreman, with a *remuda,* or pool of saddle horses, a chuck wagon loaded with supplies and blankets, and—very important—a cook. A roundup boss was elected, who assigned to each team a certain area from which they were to drive all the cattle they could find to a central gathering place.

As they were driven out of the canyons and brush, almost every cow had an awkward, spindle-legged calf nuzzling close to her. Each calf had to be roped and thrown so that it could be marked with its mother's brand, to show which rancher owned it. Small fires dotted the brand-

ing area, each one with several glowing branding irons in it. The branding iron was simply a
long iron rod with a symbol at its end. This
might be the letter *S* lying on its side—the
Lazy S. An *O* with a dot in its center was called
the Circle Dot, and so on. Each ranch was known
by its special brand, and all its cattle wore this
mark.

Another purpose of the roundup was to cut
out beef cattle of the right size and age to
be shipped to the stockyards. While the rest of
the herd was allowed to scatter over the range
again, the selected cattle were driven to the stock
pens at the railroad siding. There they were
loaded into cattle freight cars, built with spaces
between the siding boards to allow the animals
more air. Then they were either shipped to St.
Louis, Cincinnati, Chicago, or some other packing town to be turned into meat, or sent to a
Midwestern feeder to be fattened on corn before
being slaughtered.

These long train rides were often hard on the

47

poor animals, especially in hot or cold weather. Although they were fed and watered regularly during the trip, they always lost a lot of weight and were often bruised by the knocking around on the train and in loading. Thin, bruised cattle mean fewer pounds of good meat and therefore less profit for the cattleman, but in those days it was assumed that nothing could be done about it.

In the early 1870's there were still vast stretches of the United States hundreds of miles from the nearest railroad. Many ranches in southwestern Texas, New Mexico, Wyoming, Montana, and the Dakotas had to wait years before the rails reached them. In the meantime, there was only one way to get the cattle to market: to trail-drive the herds over hundreds of miles of wild desert and mountain country, fording swift rivers, and often fighting off Indians, cattle rustlers, and wolves.

The trail-drive map shows the famous cattle trails and the great distances traveled by the millions of cattle that passed over them. These were mostly black Texas longhorns, whose horns sometimes measured as much as seven feet from tip to tip. These descendants of the Andalusian cattle brought over by the Spanish explorers centuries before were well suited to the rough life of the dry Texas plains. They could fight off wolf packs, swim swift rivers, and survive bad droughts.

The longhorns, however, were so small and wiry that they did not produce much meat, and what they did produce was very tough. But since

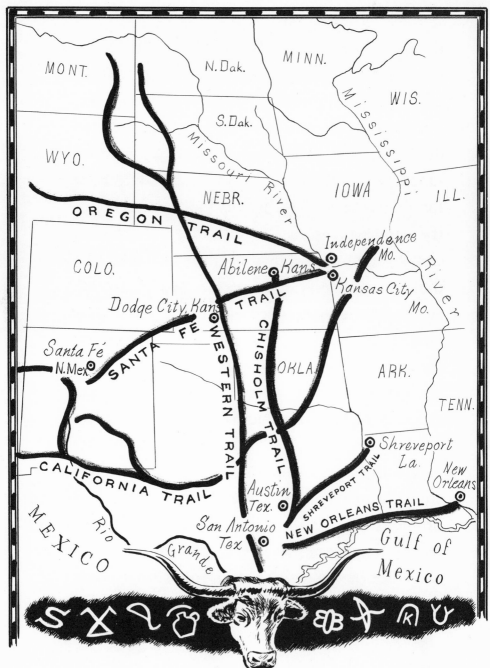

FAMOUS CATTLE TRAILS

the days of improved breeds were still in the future, the packers had no other choice. They bought the longhorns, but at low prices.

Often several ranchers joined forces in a trail drive, each of them bringing cattle from his ranch to form one big herd and furnishing men for the drive and horses for the *remuda.* Such a trail drive was an exciting thing to watch. The chuck wagons, loaded with the cow hands' bedding, tools, rifles, and harness and the cooks' supplies and utensils, led the way. There were two reasons for this: dinner would be ready by the time the rest of the expedition arrived, and the provisions would escape the choking dust raised by thousands of hoofs. Meat for the riders' meals was never a problem. Wherever they camped, the cooks simply slaughtered enough steers to provide every hand with all the steak he could eat. What could not be eaten was often left for the coyotes.

Behind the chuck wagons came the *remuda,* from which each man roped a fresh horse every morning. Without plenty of fresh horses a trail drive could get into a lot of trouble. So the *remuda* was carefully watched by the horse wranglers to see that the horses were well fed and that any lameness or other disability was treated.

Last of all came the herd, which was sometimes strung out for miles. It was flanked by cowboys, who kept the cattle from straying or lagging. Far ahead, scouts fanned out, looking for water and good camping spots for the night.

Water was terribly important; if the animals were not watered regularly, the weaker ones soon dropped down and died. Grass had to be found too. Unless the cattle had time to graze along the trail, they soon became too weak to travel.

A river crossing often meant trouble. As the herd crowded tightly along the near bank, small groups of steers were cut out and driven into the river by the yelling cowboys, to swim across and be herded on the other side. When they were all across, the drive could continue. Sometimes cloudbursts upstream swelled the rivers, and many cattle—sometimes even men and horses—drowned during a crossing.

At night, sudden storms, Indian raids, or attacks by rustlers might frighten the herd into stampeding. This was the thing most dreaded by the riders. It took days of hard riding to reassemble the cattle after a stampede and many of them were always missing—killed, strayed, or stolen. So during the long nights the cowboys on watch walked their horses slowly around the herd, singing softly to the cattle to let them know all was well. Many of the cowboy songs we hear on the radio were first made up and sung by cowboys to soothe their charges on the trail.

A trail drive was a very slow-moving affair, so it was often months on the way; but at last it reached its final night stand outside some dusty cow town with stock pens along a railroad siding. Here the cattle buyers haggled over prices with the trail boss until they came to terms. Then the cattle were driven into the pens to be shipped east, and the drive was over. After a few days' celebration, the riders were ready to face the long trip back to the home ranch.

Not long after cattle began roaming the open ranges of the West, sheep raisers found that conditions there were just as good for sheep as for cattle. They began grazing their flocks on the ranges, guarded by shepherds with their wonderful helpers—the trained sheep dogs. Soon there was trouble between the sheepmen and the cattle ranchers, who claimed first rights and complained that the sheep, which grazed much closer than the cattle, were destroying the grass roots and killing the pasturage forever. For many years sheep wars flared and smoldered; men on both sides were murdered and many sheep were destroyed. Not until most government land had been sold to private owners and each rancher stayed on his own fenced land or on government-leased land policed by rangers, did these strange wars finally come to an end.

Cattle rustling is still a problem to the ranchers. In the wild old days, a band of thieves would simply round up cattle scattered over the range and drive them to a dishonest cattle buyer, first altering the brand marks by burning new brands over the old ones. A *V*, for instance, could easily be changed to a *W*, or an *N* to an *M*. Rustlers were hard to catch, but when they were captured by an angry posse they were quickly strung up on the nearest tree or pole.

The modern rustler seldom uses horses or tries to make away with a large herd. A prime heavy steer is worth so much today that the rustler only needs to steal a few of them to make a good haul. He chooses only the best animals, loads them into motor trucks, and drives off, killing and skinning them to hide any evidence before he sells the meat.

We have seen how the means of getting meat animals to market changed, from the early New England cattle drives to the long trains of cattle cars that carried Western stock for a thousand miles to the stockyards. How did butchering and packing methods change during this time?

For a long time the packers' biggest problem was lack of refrigeration. In the early days of meat handling in this country, meat often spoiled before it could be sold to the consumer. Nobody seemed to think of cutting ice from frozen lakes and storing it in icehouses, buried in sawdust to slow down melting, and then using the cakes to chill iceboxes in hot weather.

The idea was centuries old. Maharajas in ancient India and Roman emperors used to have

snow packed in boxes and brought down from mountain peaks to cool their wine during hot weather. Yet refrigeration was not generally used until well into the nineteenth century.

Without refrigeration, the only way packers could sell fresh meat was to have their plants close to their customers. The meat they could not dispose of readily had to be salted and packed into barrels of brine. That is how meat packing got its name. Today, however, only a small amount of meat is packed in brine, mostly for use in lumber or mining camps far from good transportation, so the name is no longer really appropriate.

Early slaughtering was done by hand, without any of the machinery seen in modern plants. Almost the only by-product the packer saved was the hide, always useful for leather. In those early days much of the meat we now eat and enjoy was unwanted. The only hog products, for instance, that were profitable were hams, shoulders, sides, and lard. The pork packers of Cincinnati, then known as Porkopolis, had to throw spareribs, neck pieces, backbones, and trimmings into the Ohio River.

In the early 1870's, meat handlers began using natural ice in their plants to prevent the enormous waste due to meat spoilage. The plants built huge icehouses, often larger than the plants themselves, to store the ice cakes cut from nearby ponds and rivers during the winter, and these were used to keep the meat-storage rooms chilled. The invention of the brine tank in 1877 and the artificial ice plant in 1880, which was able to make ice all year around, made the enormous natural-ice storage houses unnecessary. The final step was the freezing plant, where meat can be frozen solid and kept for a long time. Freezing is used chiefly for pork. Most beef is simply kept chilled at about thirty-two degrees until it is put on the butcher's counter, because fresh beef has a better flavor than frozen beef.

One of the high points in the meat industry was the invention of the refrigerator car. In about 1870, when packing plants were chilling their storage rooms with ice cakes, somebody realized that it would be much cheaper to ship dressed meat to the branch slaughterhouses than to ship live animals, only half of whose bulk represents usable meat.

Something, however, had to be devised to keep the meat from spoiling en route in the freight car. So the first refrigerator car was built—a box-

car equipped with double walls filled with sawdust or other insulation, and with bins that could
be loaded with ice cakes through a hatch in the
roof. The first cars had long bars running length-
wise under the roof, on which the beef quarters
and dressed hogs were hung from hooks.

The ice kept the cars so cold that the meat did
not spoil, but when they were sent on their way
difficulties arose. The first car to arrive at the
Hoosac Tunnel in New York State stuck fast in
the tunnel. The eaves of the car roof were so
wide that the car could not get through until
they were sawed off. Then the railroad men
found that the movement of the train made the
long rows of beef quarters and hogs begin to

swing. By the time the train hit a sharp curve those thousands of pounds of swaying meat often tipped a car over and derailed it.

The improved refrigerator cars of today stay on the rails. They are cooled before being loaded, and the ice is mixed with salt in order to make it melt faster and so keep the car colder.

The Meat Industry Today

The refrigerator car changed the whole picture of the meat industry. Slaughtering is no longer chiefly a winter activity. The packers can now slaughter animals all year long and ship their fresh meat long distances to their branch houses even during the hottest weather. From there it goes to the retailers of each area in refrigerated trucks. Even in districts without branches the packers are able to give complete service by switching the refrigerator cars to a sidetrack from which the trucks can take their loads of meat.

The whole process of raising and distributing meat has become a very scientific operation. Old-time stockmen and packers would hardly recognize their business today. Science enters at the very beginning, with irrigation, the study of soils and seeds, and the crossbreeding of grains and grasses, to make sure that the animals will get the proper diet to make them heavy and their meat tender and juicy.

Breeding the right animal for the range he is to grow on is no longer guesswork. Some stock must withstand intense cold, others great heat, and still others high altitude. Some ranges are subject to long droughts and in others insects are a serious concern. The breeder now "designs" his animals to fit the special conditions they will have to face.

1. Cattle

Because grass-fed cattle do not produce beef as tender and juicy as that of corn-fed animals, most beef cattle are no longer shipped direct from the grass range to the packer. After a good start on the range, they are sent to Middle Western feed lots on farms that raise a lot of corn and other grains and fodder. Here they are given all the rich feed they can eat until they are heavy enough to be sent to the stockyard where they are butchered.

Today every last scrap is used for food or by-products. There is no longer anything left to throw away. Storing the meat in chilling rooms or freezers and distributing it by refrigerator cars, ships, and trucks to retail stores assures the availability of every kind of meat all over the country during every month of the year.

Now let us take a closer look at the breeding and raising of meat animals, both for quality and quantity. Our early cattle were descendants of Spanish, English, or Dutch cattle. The European cattle of those days were generally of very poor quality. During Queen Anne's reign in England, London beefsteak clubs were as popular as coffeehouses, but the beef was so tough that a gentleman riding to his club for a steak dinner sometimes slipped a steak between the

saddle blanket and the saddle and tenderized it by jouncing on it as he rode in to London.

Cattlemen finally realized that no one breed of cattle is equally good for all purposes. Some kinds give more and richer milk than others, so dairymen built up their milk herds from strains such as Ayrshire, Brown Swiss, Guernsey, Holstein-Friesian, and Jersey. A good milker is not necessarily a good beef animal, however, so the beef ranchers and farmers had to find other breeds. Although the old Texas longhorn was strong and hardy, it was too small and stringy to make good beef. So it has disappeared, except for a few small herds kept by some of the great ranches as a reminder of the adventurous days of the trail drive.

Today's beef cattle usually belong to one of four breeds: the Shorthorn, the Hereford, the Aberdeen Angus, and the Santa Gertrudis. The Shorthorn, first brought from England in 1783, is the largest and most widely distributed of the beef breeds in America. Shorthorns vary in color

BRAHMA BULL
AND SANTA
GERTRUDIS SON

from all red to all white, with red-and-white combinations in between. They have thick loins and large hindquarters, which produce the higher-priced cuts, and they make a high grade of beef.

HEREFORD

ABERDEEN ANGUS

The Hereford was brought from its native Herefordshire, in England, by Henry Clay in 1817 and soon became a favorite of the western ranchers, because it, like the longhorn, was able to forage for itself in rough country. The Here-

SHORTHORN

ford has a red body with a few white markings and an all-white face. This breed is sometimes called the Whiteface. The body is low and blocky and it fattens easily into a large quantity of good beef.

The Aberdeen Angus comes from Aberdeen County in northeastern Scotland and was introduced here in 1873. The Angus is a glossy solid black in color and has no horns. Smaller than the other beef breeds, it fattens easily while young and so makes the best baby or yearling beef.

The Santa Gertrudis is a very interesting example of crossbreeding. It was developed through experiments carried on by the famous King Ranch, a great beef empire of 940,000 acres in southern Texas. Ranchers in the hot, arid Southwest found that the beef breeds imported from cool, damp England and Scotland did not do well there, so they brought in Brahma bulls from India. These odd-looking, wide-horned cattle with humps on their backs were accustomed to a very hot climate and insect pests of all kinds. When Brahma bulls were bred with English Shorthorns, a new breed resulted and was named the Santa Gertrudis. This animal, a deep cherry-red in color, kept its father's ability to stand heat and drought, but produced the same high-grade beef as its Shorthorn mother. It is now one of the favorite breeds of the Southwest.

When a calf is born on the range it stays with its mother until it stops nursing and begins to eat grass. At the roundup where it is branded it may either be cut out of the herd and shipped to market as veal or left on grass to grow larger. At a later roundup the rancher may decide to sell the young animal to a Midwestern feed lot or, depending on market conditions and pasturage, he may leave it on the range another season to mature and then sell it direct to the stockyard.

The cattle sold to the feed lots are in for a real cow paradise—for a short time. There they are encouraged to eat all the corn, soy meal, and other succulent fodder they can hold. In Florida,

71

where cattle raising is a rapidly growing industry, they are fed orange and grapefruit rinds from the juice-freezing plants, mixed with molasses and other ingredients and fortified with vitamins. This diet seems to work out very well for the cattle and uses up a lot of useless citrus rinds profitably. After the animals have had nothing to do but rest and eat for a few months, their ribs disappear and they become solid and chunky.

Now it is up to the feeder to try to guess the best time to ship his beef to market. If he waits awhile, perhaps beef prices will rise; but then again they may drop, and in the meantime those cows and steers can eat a staggering amount of expensive corn and fodder. If he is lucky he will make a good profit on each animal; if he guesses wrong he may get less for the "finished" steer than the sum he paid for it plus the cost of feeding.

Once the cattle arrive at the stockyards, a commission man (so called because he gets a percentage of what the rancher receives) takes charge and acts as the cattleman's agent. He aims to sell his beef to a packing-house buyer at the highest price possible. The price per pound he gets will depend upon the current scarcity or abundance of animals in the yard and upon the grade of his beef.

The cattle buyer is such an expert that he can tell, just by looking at it, almost exactly how many pounds of usable meat will come from a

steer and what grade the meat will be; that is, its flavor, tenderness, color, firmness, and amount of fat.

Beef is divided into seven grades. The top quality is called prime; next comes choice, then good, followed by utility, bulls, cutter and canner, and the lowest grade, commercial, which is used chiefly for canning.

Here is what happens to a 1000-pound steer. The packer slaughters and dresses the carcass, which by this time has shrunk to 590 pounds in weight. This doesn't mean, though, that the other 410 pounds are wasted. They represent the by-products—hide, fat, hair, and organs—which will all be put to good use.

The retail butcher cuts up the carcass to make the following retail cuts:

Porterhouse, T-bone, and club steak	35 lbs.
Sirloin steak	55 "
Round steak	50 "
Rib roast	30 "

Boneless rump roast	25 lbs.
Chuck roast	105 "
Hamburger	100 "
Stew meat and miscellaneous cuts	50 "

This comes to 450 pounds of usable meat; waste and trimmings amount to 140 pounds. The butcher was able to carve only 90 pounds of sirloin and porterhouse steak from a 1000-pound steer. As long as most people prefer steaks and roasts, butchers must charge relatively little for the other cuts in order to tempt somebody to buy them. They make up for this by upping the prices of the popular cuts.

In the early days of meat packing very little was known about the value of by-products or how to use them; until the middle of the nineteenth century very little profit was made from their sale. In the 1880's scientists finally began to work in earnest to try to cut some of the waste in the process of meat packing. Steadily their work grew more and more successful, until today most of the profits of meat packing come from the sale of the by-products.

2. Sheep

The sheep was one of the first animals to be tamed and domesticated by man. Columbus took sheep with him on his second trip to the West Indies, the Spanish explorers had flocks in their

expeditions, and the English colonists imported sheep as soon as they could take care of them.

Large numbers of sheep are raised in the West and Southwest, in great flocks which wander over the range, feeding wherever the grass is good, then moving on to fresh pasturage. Some flocks range over public land, their owners paying a fee for the privilege. Others stay entirely on private ranges, and still others do both.

Sheep are usually watched over by shepherds, one or more to each flock, who stay with the sheep twenty-four hours a day. Some of them live in small chuck wagons, but many just pitch a tent wherever the sheep bed down for the night. Shepherds are often Basques, natives of the mountainous border between France and Spain. They seem to understand sheep better than most people do, and they don't mind the loneliness of the job.

Each shepherd has his indispensable dog, without which he would be almost helpless. The sheep dog is so well trained that it seems almost as if he could take care of the flock without his master. When the flock is on the move, he circles the sheep, driving them in the right direction by barking and lunging at them and nipping the heels of any animal that tries to stray. At night he is always on the alert for prowling wolves or

Leg
Loin
Rib
Breast
Shoulder
Shank
Neck

SUFFOLK
EWE

RAMBOUILLET
RAM

DORSET
RAM

OXFORD DOWN
RAM

mountain lions, which hang about the fringes of the flock hoping to cut out a juicy lamb.

Today 600,000 ranches and farms in all parts of the United States raise some sheep, but the center of the industry is in southwestern Kansas, where the Rambouillet, Columbia, Corriedale, and Panama strains are the favorite breeds. Many small farmers keep a few sheep, fencing them into pastures too rough to mow and so making use of forage that would otherwise go to waste. These small flocks are usually one of the Down breeds: Hampshire, Oxford, Shropshire, Suffolk, or the famous Southdown, which all came originally from the British Isles. All these breeds are hornless and have dark faces and legs.

3. Hogs

Pork, the meat of the hog, is eaten in almost every country except those where religious laws forbid it. The Chinese, the Dane, the German, the Scot, and the South Sea Islander all enjoy it—as roast pig, pig's feet, or pork chops, as juicy hams, bacon, or crisp pork sausage. The ancient savage Briton feasted on acorn-fattened pigs from the oak forests, and pork was a favorite dish at Roman banquets.

The early American colonists always had a pig-pen behind the barn, and they depended heavily on salt pork during the long periods when they could get no fresh meat. Even today a pig or two being fattened for slaughter in the fall spells the difference between a full plate and actual hunger to peasants and poor farmers all over the world. Salt pork was the mainstay of Washington's armies during the Revolution and of the frigates' and clipper ships' crews during the great days of sail.

There is one big reason why more pigs are raised the world over than either of the other two leading meat animals: a pig can be kept in a small pen. Pigs digest their food very much as we do, so they can be fed on grain and scraps.

DUROC-JERSEY
BOAR

HAMPSHIRE
BOAR

BERKSHIRE
BOAR

CHESTER WHITE
SOW

This means that they require very little room. Cattle and sheep, whose four stomachs can turn grass into nourishing food, are grazing animals (grass-eaters) and need many acres of pasturage.

In countries with dense populations, like China or India, every inch of tillable land is needed to grow rice or other cereal grasses. Pasture land is too expensive a luxury, and so there is no beef or lamb; pork is the only meat.

Just as intelligent breeding of cattle has provided us with good beef, similar breeding of hogs has brought us tender pork and ham. The thin, tough razorback that once ran wild in the piny woods now supplies the highly prized Smithfield ham of Virginia. Other wild hogs have been changed into fat, sleek porkers that live in clean pens and have their meals planned and served almost as carefully as if they were house guests.

Today most hogs belong to the Poland-China, Berkshire, Chester White, Hampshire, Duroc-Jersey, Hereford, Tamworth, or Yorkshire breeds. Much of our pork comes from small farms that fatten only a few hogs a year, but there are also many breeders who raise very large herds. The center of the hog-raising area is Iowa and Nebraska, where the farmers raise enormous corn crops that bring the most money by being converted into pork.

Here is what becomes of a 240-pound hog that has been stuffed with corn, soybean meal, peanuts, and other delicacies. At the packing house he is turned into a dressed carcass weighing 180 pounds and consisting of unprocessed fresh meat and fat. Some of the meat cuts will weigh even less after they are boned, cured, smoked, and pickled. By the time the meat is ready to be sold by the butcher, there will be only 150 pounds of it. This consists of:

Ham	29 lbs.
Bacon	27 "
Pork Roast	18 "
Small picnic hams and smoked butts	11 "
Center-cut pork chops	10 "

Pork sausage	8 lbs.
Miscellaneous cuts	5 "
Salt pork	7 "
Lard	35 "

Only 10 pounds of pork chops from a 240-pound hog! Like beefsteaks, pork chops are high-priced because everybody wants them. The butcher charges less for the less popular cuts to get rid of them, and he makes up the loss by charging more for chops, ham, and bacon.

Inside the Slaughterhouse

What actually happens in the modern slaughterhouse into which so many millions of meat animals are led every year? Turning a live steer or hog into steaks and chops is a complicated job. It is a long jump from the days when the butcher hoisted the beef carcass by slinging a rope over the nearest tree limb in the orchard and then, while he worked, had to keep shooing away all the dogs within five miles.

Let's follow the progress of a chunky 1400-pound Shorthorn steer, just bought by the packing-house buyer and waiting, unaware of his fate, in the pens. He is led up a winding ramp to the fifth and top floor of the packing house and into a narrow pen. From this point all his progress will be downward until he finally leaves, as a side of beef, from the ground floor.

First he is stunned by a quick blow on the head with a sledge hammer and thereafter knows no more. Next one side of the pen drops down and he slides down to the floor, where both hind legs are shackled to a chain and he is hoisted to a trolley on an overhead rail. Here the unconscious animal's neck arteries are severed and his blood flows into a tank and is saved.

Now the skinning team takes over and, with a few swift, skillful strokes of the razor-sharp skinning knife, removes the hide undamaged and in one piece. Next the internal organs are removed and Federal meat inspectors examine them as well as the glands and the entire carcass. The steer has already been inspected while alive; this check is even more careful. Any sign of disease found along the disassembly line means that the carcass will be removed and placed in a tank as unfit for food and useful only as fertilizer or for some other safe purpose.

When the carcass has been approved by the inspectors, a man with an electric saw cuts part way down the spine, then finishes splitting the carcass halfway down its length with a long-handled cleaver. Next it is thoroughly washed with jets of hot water and incased in a tight muslin bag, which gives the flesh a glossy finish. Still

steaming, it is rolled into the chilling room to be cooled and hung up. There it waits its turn to be shipped by refrigerator truck or railroad car to a branch house or dealer, and from there to the butcher, who will trim it into the familiar cuts you see on his counter.

Only the higher grades of meat get to the butcher shop in the form of carcasses. Although the lower grades are perfectly good and nourishing, they are less tender. They will be turned into canned meat, sausage, or frozen meat.

Now let us see what happens to the rest of our steer. Some of the organs, such as the heart, liver, and tongue, make fine eating; they follow the carcass to the meat shop. Others will be used as sausage casings or part of the sausage stuffing itself. Part of the fat becomes oleomargarine or shortening for frying and baking. Some of the bones, sinews, and fat are ground up to put into animal and poultry feed, and the rest becomes plant food and fertilizer.

The hide, weighing about 70 pounds, will

by-products

make fine shoes, wallets, belts, and handbags after it is tanned and treated. The hair from the tail will be used to stuff upholstered furniture and the fine hair inside the ears makes artists' brushes.

The tallow from the steer's fat helps to make soap and glycerine as well as many of the new plastics, and the bones are ground up for glue and bone meal. Artificial rubber, resins, lubricants, explosives, cosmetics, paints, waxes, and many other products are made from the remaining grease, bones, hair, and blood of this very useful steer.

Even more important than these by-products, from the standpoint of our health, are the drugs and medicines which research scientists have learned to make from the glands and livers of meat animals. Insulin made from the pancreas saves the lives of millions of people with diabetes and makes it possible for them to live normal lives. Liver extract helps those who suffer from anemia, and thyroid extract has many uses. The animal's pituitary glands supply hormones used in making cortisone and ACTH, which help victims of arthritis, rheumatic fever, gout, and asthma. Each year more and more useful medical products are being discovered—all from what was once packing-house waste. From horns to hoofs, every last bit of usefulness has been squeezed out of these 1400 pounds of steer before the packing house has finished with them.

Turning a live hog into pork is only slightly different from getting beef from a steer. When the hog arrives at the top of the ramp, he, too, is hoisted to an overhead rail, and is quickly dispatched and bled. Then his carcass is wheeled along to the scalding vat, where it is plunged into hot water until the hair is loosened. Next it is attacked by a scraping machine, which removes the hair with revolving scrapers while more hot water is sprayed on it. As the carcass passes through a burner built to conform to its outlines, the remaining fine hair is singed off.

Now the pink carcass is beheaded and cleaned.

Then it is split down the exact center of the backbone with a wide-bladed chopper handled by a real expert. Unless the split is exactly centered, the two pork loins will be unequal in size and the weaker one will probably break and so bring a much lower price.

Next the leaf fat is pulled from the carcass; this will be turned into high-grade lard. At this point the carcass is often cut into hams, shoulders, loins, back, belly, spareribs, fat back, and plate. Each cut is inspected, and if O.K.'d it is marked with a stamp of purple vegetable dye by a government inspector, as "U.S. Inspected and Passed." The fresh meat is then hung in the chill room until it is to be shipped out, while the ham, bacon, sausage meat, and other specialties are salted, seasoned, smoked, or cooked according to the packer's jealously guarded secret recipes.

We get from pork many of the same by-products as from cattle, and the packers overlook none of them. There is truth in the saying that the pork packer uses every part of a pig except his squeal.

About the Author

WALTER BUEHR was born in Chicago and studied art in Detroit, Philadelphia, and New York. A well-known commercial artist, he has also written and illustrated several previous books for young people and contributed many articles to magazines featuring home design. He served with the first camouflage section at the front in World War I and has traveled widely. His interests range from sailing (he lives aboard a 43-foot cutter in summer) to the designing of furniture, ceramics, and high-fidelity systems. His home is in Darien, Connecticut.